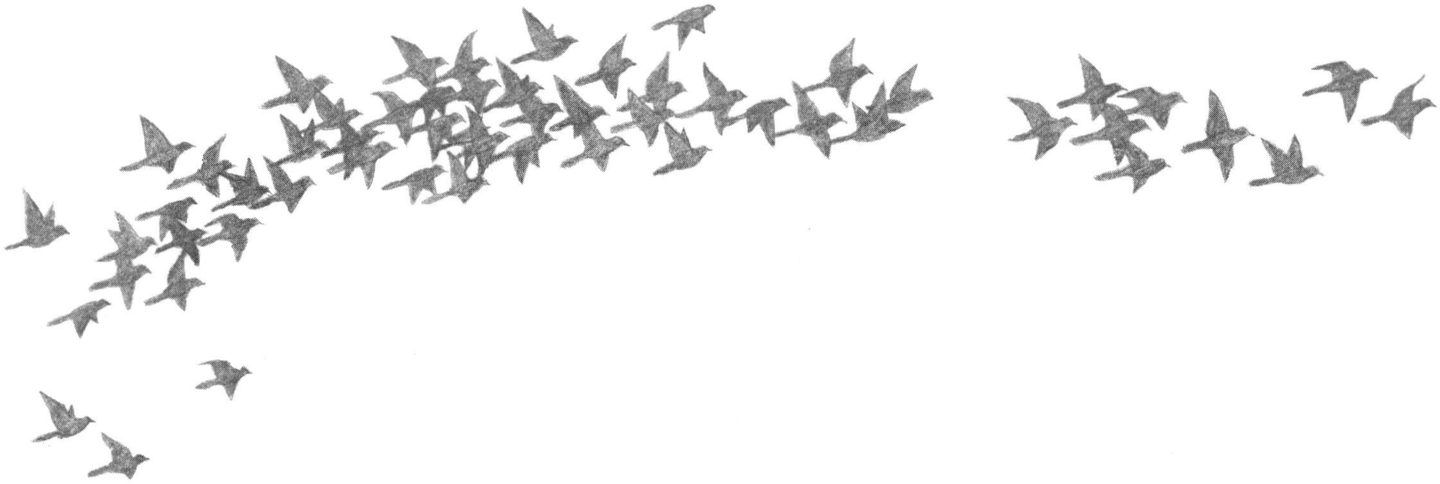

Album of Birds

By TOM McGOWEN
Illustrated by ROD RUTH

RAND McNALLY & COMPANY
Chicago · New York · San Francisco

For Carli and Tiffany

**Text and illustrations reviewed and
authenticated by Dr. John Fitzpatrick,
Assistant Curator of Birds,
Field Museum of Natural History,
Chicago, Illinois**

Library of Congress Cataloging in Publication Data

McGowen, Tom.
    Album of birds.

    Includes index.
    Summary: Discusses the evolution of birds from
reptiles, the way of life of different types of birds,
the adaptation of species to their niches, the care of
baby birds, and migration.
    1. Birds—Juvenile literature. [1. Birds] I. Ruth,
Rod, ill. II. Title.
QL676.2.M39 1982   598   82-9128
ISBN 0-528-82413-9   AACR2
ISBN 0-528-80076-0 (lib. bdg.)

First printing, 1982

Contents

Birds—Descendents of Reptiles

SOME 140 MILLION YEARS AGO, a creature sat on a branch of a ginkgo tree not far from the edge of a sea. The sky was gray and overcast, and a wind was rising. A storm was about to break. The wet, sandy shore was dotted with the huge footprints of a herd of gigantic long-necked, long-tailed reptiles that had passed by a short while before. This was the Age of Reptiles—the time of the dinosaurs.

The creature on the tree branch was like nothing that can be seen today. It was clearly a bird, with feathered wings and a long feathered tail. But its head was like the head of a lizard, with jaws studded with tiny sharp teeth. And at the end of each of the creatures wings was a three-fingered claw.

The birdlike creature launched itself from the branch and, with wings stiffly outstretched, began a long glide to another tree some distance away. But at that moment the rainsquall struck. There was a sudden wild surge of wind filled with driven, stinging raindrops. The wind caught the flying creature and whirled it out over the sea.

The creature awkwardly tried to flap its wings and steer itself back to the beach. But it was not a skillful flier and succeeded only in completely losing control. It went somersaulting into the shallow water. It struggled desperately for a time, then its feathers became waterlogged, and it sank beneath the surface. Its limp body drifted slowly downward and settled on the muddy bottom of the sea.

8

With time, the creature's soft parts decayed, leaving only bones and feathers. Slowly, these remains were covered with mud that drifted down in billions of tiny particles from the surface of the sea. As the mud grew thicker and heavier, the creature's remains were pressed into it by the weight.

Hundreds of years, thousands of years, millions of years, went by. The sea had dried up, and its muddy bottom had hardened into the kind of rock called limestone. The creature's bones and feathers had long since rotted away. But where they had been, their *impression* remained—like a footprint made in wet concrete, still there when the concrete hardens. And in the year 1861, workers cutting stone out of the ancient lake bot-

9

ARCHAEOPTERYX

tom uncovered this impression on a slab of rock—the impression of a crow-size creature with a lizard's head, a long snaky tail, and feathers.

Scientists who studied the impression named the creature *Archaeopteryx*, which means "ancient wing." Because it had feathers, *Archaeopteryx* is regarded as the oldest-known bird. For, birds are the only members of the animal kingdom that have feathers. However, if *Archaeopteryx* had not had feathers, scientists would have felt sure it was a small dinosaur. That's exactly what its skeleton looks like.

No remains of any feathered creature older than *Archaeopteryx* have ever been found. Thus, scientists reason there were no feathered creatures in the world until some time between 200 million to 150 million years ago. Where, then, did the feathered creatures, birds, come from? The answer is that they are the descendents of a creature that is very different from a bird—a creature we call a reptile.

Around 200 million years ago, the main sort of larger animals living on the land were reptiles—creatures like the lizards, snakes, turtles, and crocodiles of today. A reptile is an animal that has certain characteristics, or features. For one thing, all reptiles have scaly skin. So do most fish, of course. But fish breathe water, while all reptiles are air breathers, even those that live in water, such as sea turtles. Most reptiles hatch from eggs that have leathery or rubbery shells. These eggs are always laid on land, never in water like the soft, blobby eggs of fish or frogs. It is basically

those three things—having scaly skin, breathing air, and hatching from a hard-shelled egg—that make a reptile a reptile.

There were a great many more kinds of reptiles in the world of 200 million years ago than there are now. One kind were small, slim, long-tailed creatures that ran about on their two back legs and used their front legs as hands to snatch up insects and smaller reptiles. These fast-moving hunters were the ancestors of the dinosaurs, and most scientists think they were also the ancestors of birds. They believe that during the next 60 million years, some of this reptile's descendents became such creatures as the big, flesh-eating dinosaur *Allosaurus*, while others became such creatures as the feathery *Archaeopteryx*. Some scientists, however, think that a dinosaur was actually the ancestor of birds—and that birds are thus really a kind of dinosaur, too!

Whether or not they are dinosaurs, birds are definitely the descendents of reptiles and still have many of the features of their reptile ancestors. They lay hard-shelled eggs, as reptiles do, and they are all strictly air breathers, as reptiles are. Birds' feathers are formed of the same substance as reptiles' scales, and most birds' feet are covered with scales similar to those of reptiles. In fact, if you ever get the chance to compare the taloned foot of a flesh-eating bird, such as a hawk, with the taloned fossil-skeleton foot of a flesh-eating dinosaur, such as *Allosaurus*, you'll see they're very much alike. Of course, birds have bills and beaks—but so do

10

Reptiles

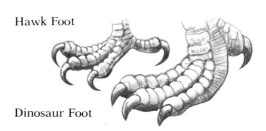

Hawk Foot

Dinosaur Foot

Archaeopteryx

some reptiles, such as the hawksbill turtle, and so did several kinds of dinosaurs. There are many bird-reptile similarities.

Why did some reptiles become feathered creatures? Simply because nature is always at work improving plants and animals, and feathers are an improvement over scales. The scaly body of a reptile is more or less at the mercy of its surroundings. It will become just as cold or just as warm as the air or water around it. And a cold reptile is at a great disadvantage because it becomes sluggish and slow moving and can't catch food easily *or* get away from something that wants to eat *it*. But feathers hold body heat in, so that a feathered reptile would have been able to stay warm and quick moving. Birds are always quite warm. In fact, by human standards they have a high fever!

At any rate, between 200 and 150 million years ago, some kinds of reptiles slowly evolved into warm-blooded, feathered creatures. These may have been reptiles that were still running around on the ground, or they may have been reptiles that climbed about in trees, leaping from branch to branch. Whichever they were, they probably had feathers for a long, long time—millions of years—before they became able to fly.

Some scientists think that even *Ar-chaeopteryx* was not yet able to fly or even glide. They think it ran about on the ground, using the long feathers on its arms to sweep insects and small reptiles into its mouth. But most scientists feel sure that *Archaeopteryx* was much like many birds of today—that it perched in trees and could at least glide, although it probably couldn't fly very well.

By the end of the Age of Reptiles, some 70 million years after *Archaeopteryx's* time, a number of different kinds of birds had appeared. One was a 6-foot-long, heavy-bodied creature with big feet and a long bill containing tiny sharp teeth. Named *Hesperornis*, meaning "western bird," it was a water dweller that could swim and dive very well and probably ate fish. However, it had only tiny, useless wings and could not fly. Another bird—called *Ichthyornis*, or "fish bird"—was about 8 inches long and somewhat resembled a present-day gull. It, too, had teeth in its bill; but unlike *Hesperornis*, it was able to fly.

By about 55 million years ago, many kinds of birds like those we know today had arrived on the scene. The dinosaurs were long gone, but these small, feathered creatures that may be their descendents, and certainly are their relatives, had spread out and covered the earth.

Ichthyornis

11

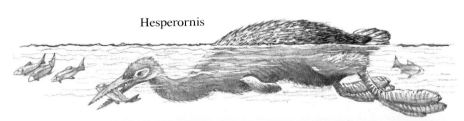

Hesperornis

Magellan Penguins

Many Ways of Life

IN THE BRIGHT, CHILL WATERS of the sea surrounding the ice-covered continent of Antarctica, a group of creatures swims steadily along beneath the surface. True sea creatures, they have been swimming effortlessly and tirelessly, mostly underwater, for hours. They are far from land and may not come in sight of land for weeks. Of course, this really doesn't matter much, for the sea is their real home and it is where they get their food.

What are these sea creatures—fish? Dolphins? No, they are birds—the birds called penguins. Penguins don't know what a tree is and cannot fly a bit. But they are marvelous swimmers that can stay underwater for as long as an hour and that often stay in the water, out at sea, for months. This is their way of life.

On a sandy African plain dotted with low bushes, a creature is running. It is a large creature, with a big body and big sturdy legs, and it weighs a good 340 pounds or more. But despite its size and weight, it can run very fast when it wants to, as fast as 40 miles an hour. Running about on the sandy plain, this big creature often goes for days without drinking any water. What is it—a camel, perhaps? No,

it is a bird—the bird we call an ostrich. An ostrich cannot fly at all but spends its days trotting in a sandy, treeless desert or a grassland dotted with trees here and there. This is its way of life.

Lots of people think of birds as flying creatures that spend most of their time in trees and eat mainly seeds or insects. But a great many kinds of birds have ways of life very different from the seed-and-insect-eating tree dwellers. While most kinds of birds are fliers, many hardly ever fly and some simply can't fly. While many birds do live in forests or wooded areas, some birds live in treeless deserts, on treeless plains, on treeless rocky mountainsides and shores, on treeless sandy beaches, in water, and even on ice and snow. And while many birds are seed, fruit, and insect eaters, others eat such things as flower nectar, honey, tree sap, acorns, fish, frogs, mice, rabbits, clams and oysters, snakes, lizards, young crocodiles, turtles, monkeys, other birds, bird eggs, and even the dead bodies of large animals.

A good many kinds of birds spend all or most of their life on the ground. This is where they find their food, make their

Male Ostrich

Female

Young

12

nests, rear their young, and where many of them hide when they are in danger.

Some of these birds—such as the pheasant, partridge, and lark—are good fliers; some, such as the roadrunner, are very poor fliers that seldom, if ever, fly; and some, such as the African ostrich and Australian emu, can't fly at all.

The food of most ground-dwelling birds is found on the ground—seeds, fallen berries and fruit, insects, and if the bird is big enough, frogs, small lizards, mice, and even snakes. Some ground-dwelling birds get their food out of the ground. They have shovel-shaped bills with which they dig up plant roots and bulbs, or they have long pointed bills they push into soft mud or wet sand to search for worms, clams, crabs, and other creatures that live or hide in the ground.

Of course, life on the ground is a bit more dangerous, perhaps, than life in the trees. But ground birds have ways of protecting themselves. Many will simply fly away from danger, of course. Some, such as the fleet-footed ostrich, can run away. But many ground birds depend on their coloring to protect them. They are generally a brownish color, with bands and speckles of black and white. Their coloring forms a pattern that makes their bodies blend in among the browns, yellows, blacks, and whites of a clump of tall grass, reeds, or a pile of dead leaves. When a bird that is colored this way crouches absolutely motionless, it becomes almost invisible.

The way of life of a great many kinds of birds is built around water—lakes, ponds, rivers, swamps, lagoons, or the sea itself. They get their food from the water, and for many of them, being able to swim is as important as, or even more important than, being able to fly.

Many kinds of birds make their living from the sea. Some live along the coasts of continents and islands and seldom get very far from shore. Their food is mostly fish. Some of them, such as terns, are good fliers but poor swimmers. Terns will skim out over the sea and dive into the water to snatch a fish, flying up again immediately. Others, such as auks, are rather clumsy fliers but fine swimmers that spend much of their time in the water.

Other birds that make their living from the sea are both fine long-distance fliers, such as albatrosses and petrels, and fine swimmers, such as penguins. These are more truly sea birds because they are usually far out at sea, miles from land, for weeks or even months. Some flying sea birds get their food by snatching live or dead creatures floating on the water; others dive into the water to get their food. When a bird such as an albatross must rest or sleep, it simply lets itself float on the sea.

Birds that live near bodies of fresh water might be divided into two groups: swimmers and waders. The swimmers are those such as ducks, geese, swans, grebes, loons, and pelicans. The waders are long-legged birds, such as herons, flamingos, and spoonbills. All these birds eat such things as water plants, fish, frogs, water

Black Tern

insects, snails, worms, and so on. The swimmers get their food by chasing it through the water or by poking their bills into the mud underwater. The waders get their food by standing in shallow water and either sticking their heads under to delve in the mud or snatching passing fish or frogs with their bills. Some wading birds often walk on land and catch small creatures they find there.

The way of life of many birds depends upon the leaves, limbs, and trunks of trees. These birds may often run or hop about on the ground, but they aren't truly ground birds. Their true dwelling places are trees or bushes. There they find food aplenty—insects crawling on leaves or hiding under bark; fruit; tasty buds; and sap, the sweet juice that flows through the trunks and branches of leafy trees and that is the main food of the birds known as sapsuckers. Among the mass of leaves small birds have good hiding places from hawks or other birds of prey gliding overhead. A high branch is also a safe refuge from many dangerous creatures that prowl on the ground. Most of the tree-dwelling birds make their nests in trees, and they generally perch on a tree branch while sleeping.

Everyone knows that most owls are nighttime, or *nocturnal*, creatures. But among tree and ground birds especially, there are a good many birds whose ways of life are also tied to the night. Throughout most of the world, soon after sunset, nightjars and nighthawks take to the air after flying insects and even small birds or bats. In South America, oilbirds leave the caves where they slumber by day to seek palm nuts and fruit. In the forests of Asia and Australia, frogmouths hunt insects, and the strange little kiwis of New Zealand probe for worms in night's darkness. And there are others. These birds live just as many daytime birds do, but they have extra-keen hearing or special night sight that enables them to do their living in darkness.

Each kind of bird is born to its way of life. Its body is shaped for the life it leads, and "messages" implanted in the cells of its body control most of the things it does. A young bird also learns much of its way of life from its parents and passes these things along to its own young. Thus, no sapsucker can grow up to become a bird of prey, like a hawk; no bulky, ground-dwelling turkey could dive underwater for food, as a grebe does. A bird lives where and as it does because that is how nature designed it to live.

Nightjar

15

Kiwi

California Condor

Wings

IT IS MORNING in a remote, mountainous region near the coast of southern California, and the sun is well up into the sky. On a narrow cliff ledge, a late-sleeping bird has awakened, untucked its head from beneath its wing, and is rousing itself for the day.

It is a big bird, with a body as large as that of a young child. When it opens its wings and spreads them out to warm in the sun, they stretch a good 10 feet from tip to tip. This is one of the world's largest flying birds—a California condor.

After a time of soaking up sunshine, the condor's wings and body are sufficiently warm to have lost the stiffness from night's chill. The morning air has also warmed up enough by now to produce rising air currents—great sheets of heated air that move upward along the cliff faces. This is what the condor requires. It shakes its wings with a mighty rumbling noise and launches itself off the cliff. It flaps its big wings several times, then holds them fully outstretched. The warm rising air pushing on the broad undersides of the wings lifts the bird upward and carries it along. With only an occasional flap, the condor will now soar and glide for miles and miles in great sweeping circles, at a speed of some 30 or more miles an hour.

This kind of flying is necessary to the condor's way of life. It is a flesh eater, but it doesn't chase and kill to get its food. It looks for an animal that is already dead, preferably a big animal, such as a sheep, deer, or cow. Thus, a high, slow, circling flight enables the bird to look over a large expanse of land, giving it a good chance to spy the motionless body of some dead creature.

Far across the land, in a flower garden, a very different sort of bird is using its wings in a very different way. The bird is a tiny, dainty creature, no more than 4 inches long—a ruby-throated hummingbird. This bird does not soar on outstretched wings. Its wings are flapping so rapidly they are a blur, so rapidly they make the humming noise that gives the bird its name. Those wings beat as fast as 60 or 70 times a second, pushing so rapidly against the wind that the bird can actually hover, or stand still in midair. The hummingbird can also fly sideways and even backward, which no other kind of bird can do.

This type of flight, too, is a necessary

Robin

Ruby-Throated
Hummingbird

RUBY-THROATED HUMMINGBIRD

Long, Broad

Long, Pointed

Short, Pointed

Short, Rounded

part of a way of life. The hummingbird cannot walk, for its legs are tiny and weak. But it feeds mainly upon nectar from flowers, and so it has to be able to move in and out among leaves and blossoms. It stays in place close to a flower while it pushes its long bill into the blossom to sip nectar. It can only do this because of the way it flies.

Far from the flower garden, another bird is using its wings in yet a different way. It is a merlin, a kind of falcon, that has sighted a flock of blackbirds. This is a bird of prey that depends on its wings to get its food, which is mainly other birds. It flies like a streak, at tremendous speed, with quick, slashing beats of its wings.

Most kinds of birds can fly, but different kinds of birds have different ways of flying, depending much on their way of life. The shape of a bird's wings will generally show the kind of flier the bird is. Long, broad wings, like those of condors or albatrosses, indicate birds that mainly soar and glide, or else birds that fly slowly and steadily with almost lazy flaps of wings, as pelicans and herons do. Long, pointed wings belong to birds that generally make long, fast flights with rapid, powerful wing beats, seldom soaring—like merlins, peregrine falcons, swifts, and swallows. Short pointed wings, such as ducks have, tell of birds that make mainly brief, fast flights—for example, from one pond to another nearby. Short rounded wings, which many songbirds have, indicate birds that usually make short, rather slow flights after a rapid takeoff.

A bird isn't just an animal with wings; it's a creature whose whole body is designed for flying. For one thing, a bird's body is extremely light. The bones of ground-dwelling animals are mostly solid, which keeps them heavy; but the majority of birds have hollow bones, which are much lighter. The bones of some birds are actually lighter than their feathers.

A bird also has fewer muscles than most four-legged animals, and this helps keep its body light. A bird's heaviest muscles are in its chest and are attached to its wings. Those muscles are actually the "engine" that powers the bird's flight. The muscles snap the wings downward in a powerful flap that drives the bird through the air.

A bird's wing may look bulky, but it's really nothing more than a few long, slim bones. These are connected end to end and covered with a bit of skin with feathers attached. Thus, the wing is extremely light. All those feathers form a hard, smooth, broad surface that slides easily through the air edge on and lifts when air pushes on it from beneath. A bird has certain feathers on its wings that act much like an airplane's propeller and that enable the bird to move forward through the air. As the bird flaps its wings or soars, these feathers twist back and forth, constantly pushing backward at the air. This backward push pulls the bird forward—in much the same way the backward push of your foot against the ground moves your body forward.

18

Gull Skeleton

Western Grebe

Birds fly for several different reasons. One good reason is, of course, to get from one place to another. But many birds must fly in order to get food. Swifts, nightjars, and some other birds eat mainly flying insects that they snap up as they move through the air. Most birds of prey get their food by catching it while flying, and hummingbirds do all their feeding while hovering or flying.

Flying may also be a way of attracting a mate. Male birds of many kinds do a sort of flying acrobatic act in front of a female at mating time. Generally, this will attract the female to become the male's mate. And after some birds have become mates, they make looping, diving flights together, as if they were celebrating by dancing.

The fastest flier of all birds—and the fastest moving of all living creatures—is the spinetailed swift. It has been timed at a speed of over 106 miles an hour. The slowest flier seems to be the woodcock, which has been timed flying at only 5 miles an hour. You can run much faster than that!

While all birds have wings, not all birds are fliers. There are a number that can fly but seldom do, some that can't fly very well and hardly ever try to, and some that can't fly at all. A grebe can fly well enough, but it has a lot of trouble getting itself into the air. As a result, it doesn't like to fly and only does it rarely. The bird called a roadrunner not only doesn't like to fly but it really can't fly at all well. Only if a roadrunner is frightened or being chased will it take to the air, and then it flies in a rather wobbly fashion for only a very short distance, never getting more than about 10 feet off the ground.

Most members of the group of birds known as ratites cannot fly at all. This group includes the biggest of all birds, the 8-foot-high ostrich; the 5½-foot-tall emu of Australia; the cassowary of Australia and New Guinea; the South American rhea; and the chicken-size kiwi of New Zealand. The bones, muscles, and feathers of these birds are just not designed for flying. The wings of the kiwi are so tiny they're hidden by its shaggy feathers.

No penguin can fly. A penguin uses its paddlelike wings to swim with, and while this bird may look clumsy and comical walking on land, it is swift and graceful in water. A penguin swimming underwater looks as if it is flying, but in liquid rather than in air.

Emu

Cassowary

Rhea

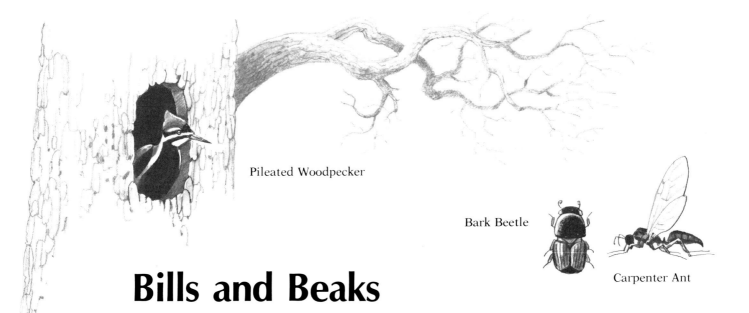

Pileated Woodpecker

Bark Beetle

Carpenter Ant

Bills and Beaks

A BIRD IS WINGING its way in and out among the trees of a North American forest. It has sooty, brownish-black feathers, and its head is adorned with white markings and a red crest like a jaunty red cap. A pileated woodpecker.

The woodpecker heads straight for an old, gray dead tree. With a quick upward swoop, it lands on the tree's trunk and folds its wings. Going easily straight up the side of the trunk, it moves about as if searching for something. Then it halts. Suddenly, there is a burst of loud, hard taps and a shower of wood chips, some as much as 3 inches long and an inch thick. The woodpecker is chiseling into the tree trunk with its sharp, strong bill.

After another quick flurry of taps and shower of wood chips, the bird pauses again. It has opened a hole like a short tunnel in the tree trunk. At the end of the tunnel lies a fat, wormlike baby beetle that has been safely protected by a thick layer of wood until now. In an instant, the woodpecker puts forth a long bristly tongue and pulls the insect into its mouth.

A great many trees in a woods are often literally filled with insects. Ants called carpenter ants make their nests in tree trunks, chewing many long tunnels in the wood. A number of kinds of beetles lay their eggs in the bark of tree trunks, and when the young beetles hatch, they live in the wood until they become adults. These ants, beetle babies, and others are a woodpecker's food. The woodpecker's bill is an efficient *chisel* for tearing open tree trunks to get at the creatures inside.

A bird's bill is actually its jaws. The bill is part of the bird's skull, but it is covered with a layer of hard stuff much the same as that covering a cow's or sheep's horns. In speaking of the jaws of birds, we sometimes use the word *bill* and sometimes *beak*. *Bill* refers to the pointed jaws of a bird such as a sparrow or a robin, while *beak* generally refers to the curved, sharp jaws of a bird of prey, such as an eagle, a hawk, or an owl. But whether a bird has a bill or a beak, its jaws generally form a marvelous *tool* that helps the bird to get or handle its food and that is often used for other things as well.

A great many birds are mainly seedeaters. A seed, like a nut, is usually covered by a tough shell, or husk; and a seedeater's bill is a very efficient "machine" for getting a seed out of its cover. The bird

20

Bill (Veery)

Beak (Bald Eagle)

Goldfinch

Evening Grosbeak

Hawfinch

takes the seed in its bill, there is a sharp cracking noise, and the husk, or two halves of the shell, come slithering out of the bill to drop to the ground while the meaty, nutritious seed is swallowed. Of course, there are tiny seeds, medium-size seeds, and big seeds, and the bills of seedeaters are suited for the kinds and sizes of seeds they eat. The goldfinch, with its little, pointed bill, eats mostly tiny seeds, usually from thistles; the chaffinch, with a larger, sturdier bill, prefers medium-size seeds; and the evening grosbeak, with a very large, powerful bill, can manage big, hard-shelled seeds. The hawfinch has such a large, strong bill that it can even split stone-hard cherry and olive seeds.

Some birds have bills that are very special tools and that sometimes have an unusual appearance. The crossbill is named after its bill, which actually looks deformed. The upper bill curves to one side, while the lower bill curves to the other, so that they cross each other. But this "design" enables the bird to easily open up pinecones to get the seeds in them.

An earthworm, sliding snugly along several inches underground, may seem to be safe from creatures on the ground above. But the bill of the woodcock is an "earthworm detector." It is long, thin, and very sensitive; and the bird, which lives in marshy, wooded places, pushes this bill into the soft earth, feeling about for worms. Even though in the ground, the bill can be opened slightly to swallow a worm. The bird known as the long-billed curlew pushes its curved, tweezer-like bill into the mud at the edges of lakes and ponds, probing for worms and shellfish. Another bird, the oystercatcher, also uses its long bill to probe in mud for worms and clams. But its bill is a chisel as well, for prying barnacles off rocks and for prying open the shells of oysters and clams.

The long, slim bill of a hummingbird is designed for getting deep down into a flower, to the sweet liquid called nectar. The hummingbird's tongue is a long, hollow "sipping straw" with which the bird sucks up the nectar.

The anhinga has a long, sharp bill that's a spear. This bird makes its home in hot, swampy places, such as the Florida Everglades, and it hunts underwater. It can curl its long neck back like a coiled spring. When it encounters a fish, it shoots its head forward, stabbing its bill through the fish's body. The anhinga then swims to the surface, gives a flip of its head to toss the fish into the air, catches the fish in its mouth, and swallows it down.

The pelican is also a fish eater that uses its bill to get its food, but in a completely different way. The underside of a pelican's bill is a large, stretchable pouch of skin attached to the bird's throat. This pouch can hold as much as 12 quarts of water, and the pelican uses its bill to scoop up quarts of seawater with fish in it. The bird then points its bill downward to let the water drain out of it and swallows the fish. Therefore, the pouched bill of a

22

Anhinga

pelican is actually a kind of fishnet.

The large bird called a roadrunner dashes about in deserts and dry parts of southwestern North America. It generally uses its long, pointed bill as a tweezers to pick up grasshoppers, tarantula spiders, scorpions, toads, and small lizards. But it sometimes uses its sturdy bill as a weapon against larger prey. For the road-runner will gladly eat snakes and will even fearlessly attack poisonous rattle-snakes, which it kills with its bill. The bird circles about, luring the snake to strike and dodging aside when it does, so that the serpent misses and finds itself sprawled out flat on the ground. At that instant, the roadrunner darts in and be-gins to hammer the snake's skull with the point of its bill until the snake is dead. The roadrunner then picks up the serpent and swallows it down headfirst.

The tailorbird of southeastern Asia uses its slim, sharp bill as a needle—and actu-ally sews with it! First, the bird uses its bill to poke holes along the edges of a large leaf. Then using both its bill and its feet, the bird pushes and pulls thin blades of grass, or strands of silk from a spider-web or cocoon, through the holes to pull the leaf edges together. This forms a fun-nel. The female tailorbird makes a nest of soft plant material inside the funnel and lays her eggs in it.

Every bird that builds a nest uses its bill to carry materials and to put them together. Birds also use their bills to scratch themselves and to smooth out their feathers. A bird will rub its bill against a gland on its back that releases a kind of oil. With its bill then covered with this oil, the bird slides the bill through all the feathers it can reach, smoothing and oiling them. This is called preening.

The beak of a bird of prey is a tool for tearing meat. The upper part of the beak is a sharp, curved hook. The falcon usu-ally uses one foot to hold down the body of the creature it has killed while it jabs its hook into the flesh and pulls, tearing off a strip of meat. Birds of prey that eat mostly other birds also use their hooked beaks to pluck their kill—that is, to pull out its feathers—before they eat it.

So, a bird's bill or beak may be used as a tool for getting food, as a pair of hands for carrying and arranging things, as fingers for scratching, as a device for smoothing and oiling feathers, and some-times as a weapon. It's a remarkable in-strument!

23

Tailorbird

Peregrine Falcon and Blue Jay

Toes and Talons

FROM A PINE FOREST on a mountainside, a streak of blue shoots skyward—a saucy, mischievous blue jay, perhaps in search of a crow to tease or an owl to annoy. An instant later, a winged blue-gray shape launches itself from the limb of a dead tree on a cliff that rises above the forest. The jay has been sighted by a peregrine falcon—a bird that hunts birds.

With quick, slashing beats of its wings, the falcon begins to gain on the jay at once, for the peregrine falcon is one of the fastest of all fliers. Staying always slightly higher than the jay, the falcon relentlessly closes the gap between them.

At the last moment, the jay becomes aware of its pursuer. Its swift, steady flight becomes a frenzied rush as it desperately tries to escape. But it is no match for the hunter. With an incredible burst of speed of its own, the falcon swoops past the jay. Its yellow, sharp-taloned foot shoots out, snatching the jay right out of the air in a grip that instantly kills it.

The peregrine falcon eats mostly birds that it kills in midair. If the bird is a jay, pigeon, or other smallish bird, the falcon usually kills it with the clutch of a taloned foot. If it is a larger bird, such as a duck or pheasant, the falcon generally dives from a great height with the three front toes on each foot curling into a ball and the sharp-taloned back toes pointing straight down like spears. The falcon strikes its prey like a bullet, stabbing the two "spears" into it and sending it plummeting lifeless to the earth.

The foot of a peregrine falcon is a deadly weapon with which the bird gets its food, and so are the feet of other birds of prey. Hawks and owls usually prey on small animals, such as mice and rabbits, which they snatch up off the ground. These birds have feet that are savage, clawed "hooks," with sharp, curved talons that bite killingly into an animal's body. The feet of an osprey, which grabs up fish as it swoops over water, are also efficient clutching hooks, with tiny spikes on the underside of the long claws to help hold on to a slippery fish. For birds of prey such as these, their feet play an extremely important part in their way of life.

The feet of birds of prey—and in fact, the feet of the majority of birds—are very much like the feet of dinosaurs! Most birds have four toes, and most dinosaurs were also four-toed animals. The most

24

Osprey

PEREGRINE FALCON AND BLUE JAY

common shape of a bird foot is with three toes pointing forward and one pointing back, just as the feet of the flesh-eating dinosaurs were formed. Some birds, however, have two toes pointing forward and two pointing backward, so that their footprints form an **X**. Some birds have only three toes, and their footprints generally form a **Y** or a **V** with a line up the middle—**V**. One bird, the ostrich, has only two toes.

Like the taloned feet of birds of prey, the feet of many kinds of birds have some special use that helps the birds in their way of life, usually in getting food. For example, wild turkeys, pheasants, barnyard chickens, and other such birds that get their food off the ground—crawling insects, fallen grain, seeds, or fruit—have feet that are "rakes." These birds will busily scratch the ground, first with one foot, then the other, raking aside leaves to uncover a crouching cricket or scratching the dirt to turn up a half-buried seed. The claws on their toes are short, sturdy, and blunt, because sharp claws would just be dulled by a lot of raking and long claws would split or break. The feet of these birds are just right for their way of life.

A bird such as a woodpecker, which has to move up and down tree trunks to get its food, has completely different feet. A woodpecker has the **X**-shaped foot. Each toe has a small, curved claw that bites down into bark, providing a tight grip. With these feet, a woodpecker can "walk," or hitch, straight up the side of a tree as easily as other creatures walk along the

ground. Its back-pointing toes keep it from slipping backward. Many other birds that have such **X**-shaped feet are also tree-trunk walkers.

Webbed feet are a big help in swimming. Many birds that spend a good deal of time in water have webbed feet. Ducks in a stream often look as if they're merely sitting in the water and letting the current carry them along. But actually the ducks' webbed feet are churning away beneath them, propelling the birds through the water. Ducks, geese, and swans, which are known as waterfowl, all have feet that are either partly or entirely webbed. Pelicans, which "make their living" in water, also have webbed feet. The water birds called grebes don't exactly have webbed feet, but their three front toes have flaps of skin on either side, making each toe a miniature paddle. Coots and phalaropes, two other kinds of water birds, have similar paddle toes.

Birds that have long, stiltlike legs—such as herons, flamingos, and cranes—are usually in water a good deal, too; but they aren't swimmers; they're waders. Those long legs enable the birds to wade or stand in fairly deep water, and their feet generally have long, spread-out toes that keep the birds' legs from sinking into the mud of a swamp bottom. Such feet and legs help the birds get their food. A long-legged great blue heron will stand motionless in water, peering down to watch for a fish, a frog, a crab, or a water snake. When one swims into range, the heron snatches it up with a jab of the bill.

26

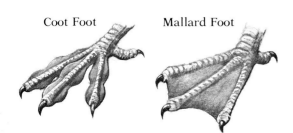

Coot Foot   Mallard Foot

Secretary Bird and Snake

The secretary bird of Africa also has long, stiltlike legs. They, too, are designed to lift the bird's body high so that it can peer down to watch for prey. However, the secretary bird isn't a water bird; it's a ground dweller that spends much of its time stalking through short grass in search of grasshoppers, small mammals, lizards, and snakes. As it walks, it often stomps its feet to startle and stir up creatures that may be lying motionless in the grass. If the bird encounters a large snake, it uses its feet as weapons, stamping and kicking the reptile to death.

Birds that spend much of their time in trees, such as robins and sparrows, have feet suited in some way to such a life. They are known as perching birds because they are able to stand on such high, thin perches as twigs, telephone wires, and other slim, rod-shaped objects. Many kinds of birds can't do this; their feet simply aren't shaped to give them a good-enough grip. But perching birds have three toes that point forward and one long one that points, or can be moved to point, straight back. The birds can curl these toes to make a tight grip around a slim branch in the same way you can curl your fingers and thumb around the handle of a baseball bat. Such a grip enables the birds, even while sleeping, to hang on to a branch swinging wildly in a strong wind.

A chimney swift has powerful wings and can stay in the air for many hours at a time. It never walks on the ground. Its food is flying insects, which it catches by simply keeping its mouth open as it flies. Thus, inasmuch as a chimney swift doesn't need its feet for getting food and doesn't use them for walking, its feet are tiny and weak. However, they do have an important use—they're hooks for hanging from. When a chimney swift wants to rest, it generally alights on a flat, vertical—or up-and-down—surface, such as the wall of a cave, the inside of a hollow tree trunk, or the inside of a chimney. Its small, sharp toenails dig into the surface like nails driven into a board, and the bird uses its tail as a prop to keep from sliding down. And there it hangs, by its tiny toes.

Some birds use their feet in ways you would never think of. When most birds fly, they fan out their tails and use them as rudders, to steer with. But the tail of the ducklike coot is too stubby for such a use. So when a coot flies, it sticks its big, fanlike, padded feet out behind it and uses them for a rudder!

27

Scarlet Tanager Gripping Branch

Chaffinch and Young

Hawk

CROWS MOBBING
GREAT HORNED OWL

Chirps, Caws, and Cackles

HIGH, HIGH ABOVE A MEADOW that spreads out from a small patch of woods, a hawk soars in slow, lazy circles. The bird is hungry, and its keen eyes are searching, searching—

High though the hawk is, another pair of rather keen eyes has spotted its silhouette. These eyes belong to a little gray-headed, pink-cheeked male chaffinch. And now, from the chaffinch comes a sound—a high-pitched *seeeeet!*

At once, several other chaffinches that are winging their way nonchalantly over the meadow turn and speed rapidly toward the patch of woods, where they can hide among the leaves. They have not seen the hawk, but they have been warned of danger by the *seeeeet* call of the chaffinch in the woods. To any chaffinch nearby, that sound means "Danger! Hide!"

Birds have a sort of "language." Each species, or kind, of bird can communicate with others of the same kind by means of what are called notes—sounds such as the *seeeeet* of the chaffinch. These sounds can be a warning, as the *seeeeet* is, or they can mean such things as "Help, I'm in trouble" or "I have found food" or "I want food" or "I am here" or "Come here" or even "Get out of here." And there are some sounds that actually seem to mean nothing less than "I'm happy."

Many birds will make a loud, shrill scream if they encounter an enemy such as a cat or an owl. This can act as a call for help, and if there are other birds of the same kind nearby, they will usually answer it. Thus, a cat or an owl may find itself suddenly "mobbed" by a flock of angry birds that are darting and swooping at it. This often drives the enemy away from the area before it can attack any of the birds that are there.

For a small bird, there are two kinds of danger. One kind moves over the ground in the form of a fox, cat, snake, or other bird-eating creature—or perhaps a curious human who is getting too close to a nest of young ones. The other kind of danger moves swiftly through the air in the form of a bird-eating hawk or falcon. So, many kinds of birds have two different danger calls. When a European blackbird sees danger on the ground, it makes a steady clicking noise that sounds like *chuck-chuck-chuck-chuck*. But if the danger is in the air, the blackbird whistles a long, drawn-out *seeeee*, much like the

European Blackbird

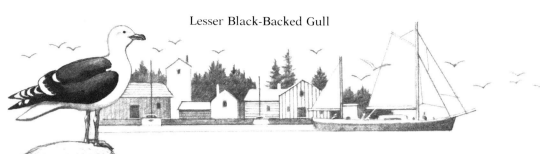
Lesser Black-Backed Gull

sound of the chaffinch. A partridge in western North America makes a sound like *whitoo* for ground danger and a sort of *kerr* for danger in the sky.

Birds of one species can sometimes learn to recognize the language of other species, especially the call that means "Danger." Thus, when a herring gull sounds a danger call, lesser black-backed gulls, which live near herring gulls, will pay attention to it. They have learned what that sound means.

Most kinds of baby perching birds that hatch in nests in trees make a begging call that means "I want food." When an adult comes to the nest, the babies beg louder and faster, with outstretched necks and wide-open bills. It's usually the baby that begs loudest and stretches its neck farthest that gets whatever food the parent has brought.

Many kinds of birds generally stay together in flocks, and these birds like to keep in touch with one another. Each bird in the flock will frequently call or twitter, and this means "I'm here." As long as a bird hears the sounds of its flock mates all around, it can't get separated from them, even though the birds may all be some distance apart and hidden from one another by tall weeds or the leaves of trees. When a flock of geese gets ready to fly, the birds make calls that grow louder and more frequent until everyone takes off. This seems to be a way of letting each bird know that the others are getting ready so that the flock will be together when it takes off.

Calls that mean "Danger," "Here I am," and so on are generally just single, rather short and harsh sounds. But many kinds of birds put a number of notes together to make an actual song—a piece of music. These are the birds we call songbirds.

The songs you'll hear from songbirds in the springtime are generally being sung by male birds, and these songs, like the call notes, actually mean something. They're a combination of an advertisement and a challenge! Each male bird picks out a territory for himself—a wide patch of land. Then, from some special high places—such as treetops or rooftops—inside the territory, he sings his song. For any females of his own kind who may be nearby, the song means "I am a bold, handsome fellow with a lot of fine land; come be my mate." But to other males of the same kind, the song means "This is my land, and I'll fight to keep you out of it!"

Daytime birds are most active in the morning and evening, and that's when they do most of their singing. Most birds begin singing near dawn and keep singing rather steadily until around noon. They're generally more quiet during the warmest part of the day, from noon until late afternoon, unless the weather is cloudy and cool. They begin singing again in the evening; and when night falls, they stop singing and sleep. On the other hand, nocturnal birds do their singing during the hours of darkness.

Songs such as the *chirdelee chirdup* of the American robin and the *wheet-cher*,

Catbird Singing

Weasel

Willow Ptarmigan

wheet-cher, wheet, wheet, wheet of the cardinal are pretty to hear. But not all birds are songbirds, and the sounds some birds make to advertise for a mate or challenge an intruder are sometimes harsh and comical. The willow ptarmigan, which lives far, far north, on the great frozen plain called the tundra, sounds a bit like a man with a scratchy, high-pitched voice, holding his nose and saying, "Go back, go back, go back!" If an intruder comes too near its territory, the ptarmigan will often charge out to do battle, making a harsh, croaking war cry that sounds for all the world like the word *tobacco* repeated over and over again. As for the famous roadrunner, it does not make a *mbeep-beep* noise, as in the cartoons; its sound is actually a sad cooing that sounds a bit like the whining of a dog.

Not all birds use their voice to call for a mate or warn off intruders. Some use sounds made by their bill or wings, instead. The European stork can make only a hissing sound with its voice, so it communicates by clapping its bill together, making a clacking noise. It uses this clacking both as a greeting for its mate and as a warning to other storks to keep away.

A pileated woodpecker and some other kinds of woodpeckers also use their bills for communication, but in a different way. A pileated woodpecker hammers its bill on a particular dead tree trunk or branch inside its territory. This makes a loud drumming sound that will carry for as much as a mile through a quiet woods. A male ruffed grouse makes a similar sound, but with his wings. He stands on a log and snaps his wings in the air, which makes a loud thump. By doing this very rapidly many times in a row, he makes a steady drumming sound. A female grouse, hearing this sound, will fly to it.

The songs of, say, half a dozen red-winged blackbirds would all sound alike to us. But just as each human's voice is a bit different from the voices of most other humans, so one bird's song or call is different from those of all other birds of the same kind. And birds can actually recognize one another by their songs or calls. When mother or father king penguins bring food to their babies, they give their call. The babies are in a huge crowd of many thousands, and there may be hundreds of parents all giving their calls—but each baby knows its parents' voices and goes right to them.

The sounds made by birds aren't merely noises. They usually have definite meanings and are made for a definite reason!

White Stork

Male Shelduck

Female Shelduck

Nest Building

IT WOULD PROBABLY surprise you to peep into a rabbit hole and find a duck looking up at you! But that wouldn't really be unusual. Mother shelducks usually make their nests deep inside old rabbit holes. For birds don't make nests only in the branches of trees, they also make them inside tree trunks, on the ground, in the ground, in caves, on cliff ledges, on the dwellings of human beings, and even on water. There are a great many different kinds of bird nests, and the kind of nest a bird makes, and where the bird makes it, depend very much on the bird's way of life and where it lives.

A bird nest generally isn't a permanent home, like the den of a fox or the lodge of a beaver. Most bird nests are simply nurseries—a place for rearing babies. Birds generally build nests when their bodies give them the urge to mate and when females will soon be laying eggs. Usually this is in the spring or early summer. Among many kinds of birds, only the female does all the work of making a nest. But among other kinds, a male and female that have chosen each other as mates will share the work. In a few cases, only the male does all the work.

Most perching birds—such as robins and sparrows—spend a good deal of time in trees. Many of them get their food mainly from trees or bushes. Thus, it's natural for these birds to put their nest in the branches of a tree or bush. Of course, they must make a nest that will keep eggs from falling to the ground. This may be just a flat platform of twigs laid in a jumble over several close branches, such as mourning doves make. It may be a more elaborate bowl- or cup-shaped nest made of twigs, grass, and mud, such as robins and grackles build. It may be a bowl with a dome of twigs laced over it to form a roof, such as a magpie constructs. Or it may be a complicated baglike nest, such as an oriole makes, skillfully woven of twigs and grass and hanging from a branch.

Most woodpeckers are tree dwellers, too. But these birds aren't perchers—their feet are made for climbing on trunks, not for gripping slim branches. So instead of making a nest among branches, birds such as the pileated woodpecker and downy woodpecker make their nest in a trunk. Using their powerful chisel bills, these woodpeckers will bore a large

32

Mourning Dove

Grackle

Great Hornbill

chamber, like a cave, in a tree trunk. They leave a pile of soft wood chips at the bottom, on which the female lays her eggs.

A number of kinds of birds will take over an abandoned woodpecker hole or a natural hole in a tree trunk for their nest. When a female hornbill of Africa or Asia finds a proper hole, she brings billfuls of mud and begins to seal it up. When it's about half-finished, she crawls inside and, with the help of her mate, finishes from there, sealing herself in. She leaves a tiny hole through which her mate can poke food. The mud dries hard, and the mother and her eggs are thus protected from snakes and other enemies. They chisel their way out as soon as the young are old enough to fly.

Perching birds and woodpeckers that live in deserts where there are no trees find substitutes for trees—usually cacti. The white-winged dove builds a loose platform of twigs among the prickly branches of cholla cacti, and the red-tailed hawk makes a ragged nest among the stubby arms of a saguaro cactus. The Gila woodpecker gouges out a nest in the side of a saguaro; and sparrow-hawks, screech-owls, elf owls, and other birds will later use this abandoned hole for their nest.

Birds that spend a lot of time on the ground usually make their nest on the ground. As with tree-dwelling birds, the nests may be very simple or very complicated. And some ground-dwelling birds don't even bother to make a nest.

When the king and emperor penguins of Antarctica aren't swimming in the sea, they walk on land. But land for them is snow. There are no trees, plants, or rocks where they live; thus, there's nothing to make a nest with. They can't use snow because that would keep their eggs too cold to hatch. And so these penguins get along without nests. The female lays her egg on the snow, then the male scoops it onto his feet and folds his belly over it to keep it warm. He then patiently stands, for *two months*, until the egg hatches!

There's usually not much material for a nest at a seashore, either. Few plants can grow in loose sand that's constantly stirred and shifted by wind. So, many kinds of seashore-dwelling birds—such as the royal tern, sooty tern, and snowy plover—either lay their eggs right on the sand or else scoop out a slight hollow and lay their eggs in that. The eggs of many seashore birds are splotched and streaked with color that makes them resemble a cluster of pebbles. Thus, although right out in the open, they are well hidden.

Birds that live in rocky places often can't make much of a nest, either. The California condor lays her egg on the bare rock floor of a cave high on cliff faces, and the peregrine falcon scrapes a shallow hollow on a narrow ledge or in a crack or hole on the face of a cliff. Guillemots, which live on rocky cliffs by the sea, lay their eggs on bare, narrow ledges often only inches away from the edge—and from a drop into the sea! Their eggs are sharply pointed at one end, so that they'll roll in a circle instead of rolling off.

34

Gila Woodpecker

Emperor Penguins

Kingfisher

But many birds that live where there is plenty of material for a nest still don't bother to make one. Whip-poor-wills live in woods, but a mother whip-poor-will lays her eggs on top of the fallen leaves on the forest floor. However, she keeps the eggs covered with her body until they hatch. She is camouflaged with colors that make her blend into the leaves, so she and her eggs are well hidden.

Many ground-nesting birds that live where there are plenty of building materials do make good use of them. The bobolink nests in grassy fields and builds a round nest made of grass and weed stems and roots. The canvasback, a kind of duck, makes a bulky nest of dry grass and weeds, hidden among tall plants near a lake or pond. The North American ovenbird lives in forests, and it builds a big bulky dome of grass, dry leaves, and strips of tree bark. These nests look a bit like old-fashioned ovens, which is how the birds got their name.

You now know that it wouldn't be strange to find a duck in a rabbit hole; but actually, other birds also make their nest in a hole. Burrowing owls, which live on plains and prairies in North America, often borrow the burrows of prairie dogs, although they can easily dig their own.

Fish-eating kingfishers dig burrows in muddy riverbanks to be close to the water where they get their food. On several islands off the coast of New Zealand, little flesh-footed shearwaters, or dovey petrels, dig burrows beneath large boulders. The mother bird and her babies often amiably share their underground nest with one of the small, pudgy reptiles called tuataras!

It might seem strange to see a bird nest on water; but that, too, is quite commonplace. Grebes are water birds that are excellent swimmers and divers but don't like to fly and can't walk well on land. They build nests that float, so that the grebes can swim to them. A male and female work together, diving down to bring up billfuls of rotting water plants. They push these together to make a large, soggy pile fastened to a plant stem or to a branch sticking out of the water. Once the pile is big enough, one of the grebes will climb onto it and stomp it into a cone shape. Such a nest rises and falls as the water in the lake or pond rises and falls. The birds called coots make similar nests.

A number of kinds of birds build nests mainly or entirely of mud. A female flamingo pushes together a squat tower of mud about 6 to 14 inches high, with a shallow scoop at the top in which she lays

35

Tuatara

Flesh-Footed Shearwater

Bald Eagle

Pied-Billed Grebe

one or two eggs. The ovenbird of Argentina builds a large dome of mud mixed with pieces of leaves and roots and with a winding tunnel inside, leading to a smooth, round room. The nest of a barn swallow is a sort of half-bowl made of about 1,000 tiny blobs of mud plastered together on a flat surface, such as a rafter in a barn or garage. The swallow makes each blob by pushing a bit of mud together at the edge of a puddle or muddy pool and carrying it in the bill to the nest. While the female pats these blobs into

place, the male goes back for another.

Birds make use of many kinds of materials for their nests, but possibly the strangest material of all is that used by some Southeast Asian swiftlets. Their nests are made entirely of saliva—spit! During mating season, the birds' saliva glands become enlarged, and their saliva becomes thick and gluey. The birds nest in caves, and they build their nests by flying at the cave wall and touching their tongue to it, leaving a drop of saliva at a time. The saliva sticks to the rock and hardens. By adding drop after drop, a swiftlet slowly builds a white, shallow cup. You may have heard of the "bird's nest soup" that some people are fond of, and you may have wondered how it was made. The soup is made from these white-saliva swiftlet nests, which are dissolved in chicken or mutton broth!

Barn Swallow

Burrowing Owl

Meadowlark

Most birds seem to build their nests in hidden places, far from other nests. And most nests are built by either one bird or a male and female together. However, some kinds of birds work together in large groups to build one giant nest they can all use. The little sparrow-size African birds called social weavers live in large flocks. At mating time the whole flock works together to make a community nest that looks like a huge pile of woven straw and dried grass hanging from the branches of a tree or the top of a telegraph pole. First, the birds make a big dome or cone-shaped roof; then they construct many tubelike tunnels, each leading straight up to a "room" under the roof. Each pair of birds has its own room, and there may be as many as 95 rooms in the whole nest.

Whether it's just a dent scooped in sand or one of the rooms in a big social weaver nest, when the nest is finished, a female bird soon lays her eggs in it. The eggs then have to be warmed, or *incubated*, so they will hatch. To do this, an adult bird crouches over them, warming them with the heat of its body. Among many birds, incubating is done only by the mother; among some birds it is done by both parents, who take turns; and among a few birds, only the male does the incubating. It may take from 11 days to 12 weeks of incubation before the eggs hatch, depending on the kind of bird.

All that time, the little bird has been forming and growing inside the egg until it fills up the entire space. One day, it begins to push and wiggle. A little point, called an egg tooth, on its tiny bill presses against the shell. The shell cracks, and the baby pushes and wiggles its way out into the nest that was made for it.

37

Social Weaver

Baby Robins

The Care of Baby Birds

HIDDEN AMONG the shaggy branches of an evergreen shrub growing on the lawn of a suburban home is a bird nest. It is a thick bowl made of dried grass and twigs mixed with mud—the nest of a pair of American robins. In the nest are three tiny, scrawny baby robins that hatched from their eggs only a few hours before. Their eyes are closed; their bodies are pink and featherless, with long skinny necks, big heads, stubby wings. They sprawl helplessly, too weak to move.

With a sudden swoop their mother arrives, landing beside the nest, on the branch to which it is fastened. Her arrival causes the nest to jiggle, and this sparks an immediate reaction among the three babies. Stretching their necks upward as far as they can, the youngsters open their bills in tremendous gapes. The mother robin is confronted with three bright red, wide-open, vibrating chasms that are squealing as if to say, "Feed me, feed me, feed me!" Into one of the yawning openings the mother stuffs the portion of worm she has brought. Then she is off in search of another worm, a young grasshopper, or some other luckless creature that can appease her babies' constant hunger.

These baby robins are completely dependent upon their parents for all their food and care and will be for quite a while. If something should happen to the mother and father robins, the weak, helpless babies would simply die.

Several hundred miles away from the nest of baby robins, three baby birds of a different kind squat in a circular nest of dried grass near the edge of a little lake. These babies, too, are only hours old, but their eyes are bright and alert, their bodies are covered with the tiny, fuzzy feathers called *down*, and they can walk quite well on sturdy legs. They are baby ducks—ducklings. Shortly, they will follow their mother to the lake where they will find they can swim quite well. While swimming, they will discover some of the things they can eat and how they can get them. After just a few days of practice with their mother, these baby birds will have a chance of surviving on their own if something should happen to her.

There are two kinds of bird babies. One kind is what is called *precocial*, meaning they are pretty well able to take care of themselves soon after hatching—like baby ducks. Precocial birds are generally

38

Ducklings

covered with down and are able to see, walk, and get their own food almost as soon as they hatch.

The other kind of bird babies is called *altricial*, meaning they are blind and completely helpless for some time after they hatch, like the baby robins and all other songbirds. Altricial birds have to stay in their nest for a long time, fed and cared for by their parents, and often have to be coaxed to fly and taught how to get their food.

For the most part, birds that hatch from eggs that are in nests high above the ground are altricial, while those that hatch from eggs laid on the ground are precocial. It's easy to see why birds that start their life on the ground have to be better able to take care of themselves right away—they're in somewhat greater danger than birds in trees or on cliffs.

Precocial birds are really quite a bit like reptiles, for baby reptiles are all able to care for themselves as soon as they hatch. Most reptile babies don't even have any help from their parents, which simply bury their eggs in sand or a pile of dried leaves or grass and then go about their business. The babies of the birds called megapodes, or mound builders, which live in Australia, start life exactly as many reptiles do. The parents scrape together a huge pile of decaying leaves and soil and bury their eggs in it. The eggs are hatched by the warmth of the pile, and the babies dig their way out and start their lives with no help. They already have feathers and fly within a few days after hatching.

But while megapode babies get no help from their parents, most other kinds of precocial bird babies get a good deal of help. For one thing, even baby birds that are covered with down lose body heat easily and have to be warmed up from time to time. The warming is done by one of the parents, which will hold the young birds under its wings and body. Thus, the babies soak up their parent's body heat. This is known as *brooding*.

In addition to being brooded, some precocial babies have to be fed by their parents for a time. Baby gulls can walk an hour after they hatch and can run within a week, but they can't fly for a month. And as gulls get most of their food by picking it out of the water while they are flying, the babies have no way of getting food for themselves until they can fly. So, their parents bring food to them. Young gulls can take up to several years to become as successful as their parents at finding food. So learning and practice are important!

But many precocial babies are able to get their own food. Baby geese and ducks can find food for themselves right away. So can baby quails, pheasants, sandpipers, and many others, but they first have to be shown how. A mother quail or pheasant will pick up a seed or berry in her bill and make a sound that causes the babies to look at her. She then drops the food and picks it up again, showing the babies what they can eat, as well as how to get food by picking it up off the ground.

Many precocial babies protect them-

Rat

selves by running away, or flying if they can, when in danger. But often, they simply "freeze," staying motionless and depending upon their color to make them blend into their surroundings. The parents of many kinds of precocial birds will usually defend their babies if need be. Some, such as the British corncrake and the lapwing, will viciously fight rats and other creatures. Terns and skuas will even try to drive off humans, pecking and striking at them. But many birds, such as the killdeer and plover, protect their young with trickery. If an intruder gets too near her nest or young, the mother lets herself be seen limping along and dragging one wing as if it were broken or injured. A dog, a fox, or even a person gets interested in following the "injured" bird and will be led far away from the young, who are sitting "frozen" against the ground. Then the mother bird takes to her wings and flies off.

Altricial birds need far more care than precocial ones, of course. They generally have to be brooded more often, until they get their feathers. And their parents may have to keep feeding them for months.

Young birds are fed in one of two ways. Among many kinds of birds, the babies get the same type of food the parents eat. Thus, robins bring their young ones worms and insects; ospreys bring fish; owls bring mice; falcons bring birds and rodents; and so on. Many baby birds simply gulp their food down in one whole piece. Robins and other insect eaters shove an entire insect into a baby's

mouth, and roadrunners do the same with lizards that are often nearly as big as the babies themselves. The parents push these headfirst down a youngster's throat; and if the lizard is much too big, its tail will hang out of the baby's mouth for a time, slowly sliding farther in as the front part of the lizard is digested.

Birds of prey, such as eagles and falcons, generally feed their babies a bit more carefully, tearing the food up for them. Peregrine falcons that bring birds to their babies tear the birds into shreds, and the babies take turns picking the shreds from the parent's beak. But as the babies grow bigger and more active, their feeding becomes noisy and wild! They stand eagerly awaiting the coming of a parent with food, and when their keen falcon eyes pick out a parent winging toward them, they break into a hopping "dance" of excitement and utter wild screams! The parent drops the dead bird it has brought, and there is a wild scramble among the young ones. Then one of them manages to pull the dead bird under itself, covering the body with its wings so the others can't get at it. They must wait until more food is brought.

The other way baby birds are fed is with food their parents have already eaten, which is partly digested. The parent forces up some of this food from its stomach and either squirts it into the baby's mouth, as hummingbirds, gulls, and herons do, or lets the baby poke its bill into the parent's open mouth to get the food, as pelicans, condors, and

40

Baby Roadrunner

vultures do. When an adult turkey vulture returns to its babies, the hungry youngsters charge with outstretched wings. The adult bird stretches its neck and opens its mouth so that a baby can push its whole head into the opening. The adult then forces up a bit of food—partly digested meat—from its stomach into the young one's mouth. This kind of feeding operation resembles a wrestling match, with the big and little birds tugging, struggling, and spreading their wings to keep their balance!

Like precocial birds, altricial parents, too, protect their young in various ways. Many of them will fly from the nest with the broken eggshells after the young have hatched. This is because the white insides of the shells could attract the attention of predators—flesh-eating birds and animals. If a predator does come near a nest of helpless young ones, most altricial parents will attack it savagely, flailing at it with their wings and pecking with their bill to drive it away. Nor are these birds the least bit fearful of attacking something far larger than they are. Even humans have sometimes found themselves being swooped at and pecked by a mother songbird who felt they were a threat to her young ones! Some altricial birds, especially those nesting on or near the ground, use the same "broken wing" trick of many precocial birds to lure intruders away from their nest full of young.

There are several kinds of altricial birds that don't give their babies any care at all. They never build a nest and never even incubate their eggs. However, they let some other bird do all these things for them!

One such parent is the mother European cuckoo. When she is ready to lay an egg, she either goes to another bird's nest and lays her egg in it or else lays the egg first and carries it in her bill to another bird's nest. After leaving her egg in the nest, she may take away one of the other bird's eggs that is already there. She generally does this while the other bird is away from the nest, and she is gone so quickly the other bird usually doesn't see the treachery. Sometimes the other mother bird or her mate will realize there's a "foreign" egg in their nest and will push it out. But, usually, the mother bird just incubates the cuckoo egg right along with her own.

When the baby cuckoo hatches, the other babies or eggs in the nest are doomed! A baby cuckoo isn't quite as weak and helpless as most other altricial babies, and it has a strong message implanted in its body. When its foster mother is away, looking for food, the baby cuckoo begins to wiggle its way around the nest. When it bumps into an egg or one of its foster mother's babies, it burrows down, loading the egg or the baby onto its back. Then the cuckoo works its way up the side of the nest and with a lurch pushes its load over the edge! In this way, the baby cuckoo wipes out all of its foster mother's young ones so that it will have the nest to itself and won't have to share food with any other babies.

The foster mother rarely seems to

Gray Jay

Bobcat

Marsh Warbler Feeding Baby European Cuckoo

realize what has happened. She feeds the young cuckoo and broods it as if it were hers. The cuckoo's foster parents may be small birds, such as sparrows, and inasmuch as European cuckoos are rather large birds, the quick-growing young cuckoo soon towers over its foster parents like a giant. Nevertheless, they still treat it as if it were their own baby. A mother cuckoo may seem like a bad parent for giving away her babies—although she's simply doing what she's evolved to do—but actually, she's seeing to it that her babies will get the best of care!

When young altricial birds have grown up enough to be able to leave the nest, their parents often use food to entice them into going. No young bird has to be taught how to fly, but many of them must be coaxed into trying to fly. Peregrine falcons will fly above their young ones, holding a dead bird just out of reach so that the young falcons must flutter up and grab if they want to eat. This makes the young ones use their wings more and more until they become confident enough to fly. It also teaches them how they will have to get their own food after leaving the nest—by snatching it out of the air.

The first week after a young altricial bird has left the nest is probably the most dangerous time of its life. It's in a brand-new world and doesn't yet know its way around. Many young birds are killed by predators or die in storms because they don't know how to protect themselves. Some even die because they cannot find food. But if a bird can survive the first few weeks after leaving its nest, it has a good chance of living a full life span.

43

Peregrine Falcon Coaxing Young to Fly

Migration

EVERY YEAR, when autumn comes to the northern half of the world, millions of birds of many kinds begin a journey. Birds of North America make their way southward to the warm parts of the southern United States or to Mexico, Central America, or South America. European birds generally move to Africa. Birds of northern Asia head for Africa, India, Indonesia, or Australia. The birds stay in these warm lands for half a year or so until spring comes to the north, then they make a return trip to the places from which they came.

In the southern part of the world, the same thing happens, but in a different direction. When it is spring in the northern part of the world, it is autumn in the southern part, and birds of southern South America, southern Africa, and southern Asia move northward. Half a year later, they return south.

This great twice-a-year journey of so many birds is known as *migration*, which means "a movement from one place to another." It is a major part of the life of many birds. They may spend many days getting ready for it and weeks or months making the trip. Some of them cover thousands of miles during the course of their journey.

Birds migrate mainly to go from where food is becoming scarce to where it is plentiful. In the northern part of the world, the coming of autumn means plants and insects will soon disappear during winter. Birds that eat such things must move to a warm, sunny place where plants still bloom and insects swarm. In the southern part of the world, much the same thing happens. Winter is a dry season, when plants wither and insects vanish. A bird such as the pennant-winged nightjar, which spends the summer in southern Africa, has to move northward into central Africa to find the water and insects it needs.

Half a year later, a bird that has migrated to find plentiful food has other needs. It is getting ready for its breeding season, when it will mate and produce eggs. The bird will need a large amount of food, both for itself and for its young. But it is now sharing a food supply with birds that regularly live in the place it is visiting, as well as with other visiting birds. So it returns to the place it came from, where spring sunshine or spring rains are

44

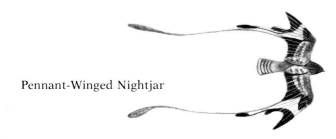

Pennant-Winged Nightjar

CANADA GEESE

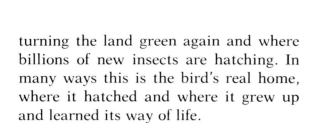

turning the land green again and where billions of new insects are hatching. In many ways this is the bird's real home, where it hatched and where it grew up and learned its way of life.

While the reasons for migrating seem obvious, some mysteries are connected with this great event in the lives of many birds. For one thing, how do birds know that food is going to become scarce? In autumn, when most birds leave the north, the weather is usually still warm and sunny, and there are flowers, fruits, and insects aplenty. How can the birds know that within a month or so most greenery will be withered, and the insects will be gone?

The birds don't know it, of course. But scientists have found that certain changes take place in a bird's body in the spring and fall, and these changes cause the bird to migrate. Thus, migration isn't something the bird thinks about or decides to do, it is something the bird has evolved to do. It must migrate just as it must eat when its body says it's hungry and just as it must build a nest when its body says it's time to breed. These kinds of built-in behaviors have been called instincts.

Another mystery is how birds find their way back to the same place each spring and fall. Some birds fly many hundreds of miles to reach a tiny, faraway place, such as a little island or a particular marsh. A human flying an airplane couldn't do such a thing without using a map, a compass, and a lot of mathematics! How do birds do it?

It seems birds that migrate during the daytime, such as swallows, have a way of using the sun as a compass. And as they near the place they are headed for, to guide themselves, they use landmarks that they remember from previous trips. As for birds that do their migrating at night, such as many kinds of thrushes, they apparently are guided by certain stars or groups of stars, just as old-time sailors were when finding their way across a sea. But for birds to be able to navigate by the sun and stars this way, they must have some built-in sense that we can't yet understand.

Birds don't all migrate in exactly the same way. Some are early starters that begin their trip in the first days of autumn or even in late summer. Others are dawdlers that stay on until the last minute. Among some kinds of birds, such as starlings, the young birds start to migrate before the older ones do; among other birds, such as red-winged blackbirds, the male and female birds start their migrations at different times. Some kinds of birds travel only by day, others fly only at night.

Some birds fly without stopping to where they are going, but most do not. A small bird, traveling mostly over land, may fly only a few hours each day, and it spends the rest of the time resting and eating. It may cover no more than about 20 miles a day and may take weeks to complete its trip. Larger birds, traveling without stopping and moving faster, may make their trip in only a few days.

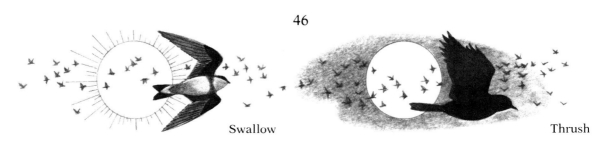

Swallow

Thrush

Willow Ptarmigan

Most kinds of migrating birds don't fly in a straight line to where they are going. Many kinds make wide detours around deserts or large bodies of water. There seem to be broad "sky paths" across parts of the world, which many kinds of migrating birds follow. However, some kinds of birds don't take the same path on their spring migration that they follow in the autumn.

For certain birds, migration is just a short jaunt of a few hundred miles, and for others it's a tremendous journey. The longest migration is made by the Arctic tern, which flies from the Arctic Circle to the Antarctic Circle—that's almost from the North Pole to the South Pole—a distance of 11,000 miles. One of the shortest migrations is that of the California mountain quail, which doesn't even bother to fly when it makes its trip—it simply walks a few miles down the mountainside. It's really just moving out of the area where heavy snow often falls in winter to the area where there won't be any snow.

A great many kinds of birds do not migrate at all. Birds that live in the tropics generally stay right where they are all year around because there is always plenty of food and life is always easy for them. However, some birds of the far north, such as the willow ptarmigan, also stay where they are all year around because they are as much at home on the frozen tundra as tropical birds are in their warm forests. During the long harsh winters, these northern birds live off the buds of trees and often take shelter in snowbanks.

A number of birds of temperate lands—places where summers are warm and green but winters are cold and snowy—are also able to survive during winters. These birds, too, stay where they are instead of heading for the warmer south in the autumn. During winter, many of them live on buds and dried berries, which are actually quite plentiful. Others, such as woodpeckers, are able to find some of the many insects that hide away in tree trunks or in the ground during wintertime.

Thus, no matter where you live or what time of year it is, you're almost always able to see birds—a great many in warm, green times and only a few in cold, gray, snowy times, but always some. And that's nice, isn't it?

Winter Bird Feeders

Barn Owl

Birds and the Balance of Nature

IN THE THICK BLACKNESS of a moonless night, a small creature moves furtively along the grassy bank of a ditch that runs near open farmland. It has a stout, furry body, pointed nose, and long slim tail. A cotton rat.

If the farmer who owns this land could see the rat, he would certainly mutter a curse at it, because this creature is one of his worst enemies. Cotton rats will eat almost anything and are thieves and spoilers of grain and other food farmers work hard to grow. A great many of these rats roam the farmer's land, and just a single pair of them can produce from 6 to 30 babies a year. If there were nothing to keep these pests in check, they could well strip the farmer's fields bare!

But there is something to keep them in check. The farmer has helpers, and one of them is perched on an old barn some distance away. It is a medium-size owl with a heart-shaped "face" and large dark eyes—a barn owl.

The rat makes hardly any noise at all as it moves through the grass. But there is enough noise for the owl's incredibly sharp ears. Slowly, the bird's head turns until its ears indicate it is facing directly toward the sounds. Then, it launches itself into the air.

The special softness of its wing feathers makes the owl's movement through the air completely noiseless, so the rat is not aware of the doom gliding toward it. Although the owl cannot see the rat, its hearing tells it exactly where the animal is. It stretches its sharp-taloned feet straight out—and strikes. Before the rat even knows what is happening, it is seized in a powerful, stabbing grip that kills it instantly.

Rats can be very troublesome to farmers. They damage and destroy crops, raid stores of grain and other food, and even kill poultry and young farm animals. Mice, too, can be troublesome. So by preying on rats and mice, barn owls and other birds of prey are valuable friends to farmers and to all of us. Because if rats and mice eat or spoil food grown for humans, we have less food and higher prices.

But, actually, birds that prey on rats, mice, pocket gophers, rabbits, and other such creatures are doing even far more important work than helping people. These birds help keep the life of the world in balance. Rats, mice, rabbits, and many

48

BARN OWL PREYING ON
COTTON RAT

Pocket Gopher

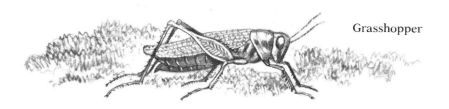

other small, furry animals preyed on by birds and other creatures can have babies at a fantastically rapid rate. And the babies of many of these animals grow up and are able to have babies of their own very quickly—in some cases, within just a few weeks after being born! If every one of these newborn animals lived to have babies of its own and those babies, too, lived to have still more babies, the world would soon be swarming with these animals! They would eat up every edible plant, seed, fruit, and nut in a countryside until nothing was left. By constantly preying on them and keeping their numbers in balance, birds of prey help stop this from happening.

Insects, too, are a constant threat to the balance of nature. There are billions of these buzzing, clicking, six-legged creatures in the world. Many are plant eaters that could destroy whole forests or lay waste to a countryside if they became too numerous. However, a great many kinds of birds eat insects, and eat a lot of them. Just one crow, for example, may eat as much as 16 bushels of insects a year. That's as many insects as could be stuffed into about 512 quart-size pickle jars! So, here again, the appetites of hungry birds help keep down the number of insects and keep things in safe balance.

Some insect-eating birds do the work of foresters, protecting trees from destruction. One of these is the pileated woodpecker, whose favorite food seems to be huge ants called carpenter ants. When a tree becomes the home of a large colony of the ants, it will eventually die as a result of their tunneling. But many a tree has been saved by a pileated woodpecker. In some way, the bird can pick out a tree that is infested with the ants and will go to work to clean out every last one.

The yellow-billed and black-billed cuckoos are also tree protectors. Most birds and animals don't care to eat hairy caterpillars, but such caterpillars are the cuckoos' favorite food. The birds are particularly fond of the hairy crawlers known as tent caterpillars, which are often seen living together in a huge, squirmy mass on the broad sheet of silk they spin in the crotch of a tree. There may be many hundreds of these caterpillars infesting a tree, and each caterpillar eats about two tree leaves a day. So these creatures can badly injure or even kill a young tree, which needs its leaves to make food for itself. Thus, the cuckoos indeed act as friends of the forest by keeping tent caterpillars in check.

What is true of the little furry animals and the insects is also true of birds. They, too, could become so numerous as to upset the balance of nature. A number of different kinds of animals prey on birds, but the most efficient bird killers are birds themselves. Hawks and owls eat some birds; and gyrfalcons, merlins, peregrine falcons, and other members of the falcon family eat mostly birds. Many kinds of birds with all-around appetites, such as crows or roadrunners, will gladly eat any bird eggs or baby birds they can get and will also kill and eat small birds if

50

Black-Billed Cuckoo

Cedar Waxwing

they can. All this helps keep the bird population in balance.

Of course, some people feel sorry at the thought of a mouse being killed by an owl or a sparrow being eaten by a hawk, but they really shouldn't. In the first place, a bird of prey has to eat, too, like every other creature, and it is designed by nature to eat flesh. This is what it *must* do to live. It is also designed to be able to kill to get its food, but it kills quickly and painlessly. It isn't being mean by doing what it does any more than you are being mean when you eat a hamburger—which is made from the flesh of an animal that was killed to make food for people!

Thus, birds that eat animals, insects, or other birds are all helping to do a job for nature. In a different way, so are birds that eat fruit. Instead of helping to keep something from becoming too numerous, these birds are helping something become more numerous—fruit trees and berry bushes. A cedar waxwing may eat several berries off a bush or vine; then it flies away. The berry seeds pass through the bird's body and are dropped in several different places where they have a chance to sprout and start new plants. A single bird may help start hundreds of new plants during its lifetime, replacing plants that have died or been destroyed. This is useful work.

There's another kind of useful work done by a group of birds that never get much credit. California condors, king vultures, and other birds that eat carrion—the flesh of animals that have died—are generally looked at with disgust. For some reason, these birds are regarded as low, mean, sneaky creatures. But actually, these carrion-eating birds are an extremely important part of the balance of nature. They're part of the earth's "cleanup crew"—birds, animals, insects, and tiny microscopic creatures that feed on a dead animal until the flesh is gone, the skeleton broken up, and the chemicals and energy of the animal's body *recycled* into the world to be used by living things. Condors, vultures, and buzzards are very useful creatures that do a worthwhile job of helping remove the world's garbage!

Like all living things plant and animal, birds are part of the great, complicated structure we call the balance of nature. Each and every kind of bird, depending on its way of life, contributes to the balance in some way and gains from it in some way.

White-Backed Vultures

More Birds

Bluebird, Eastern

For many people, the song of a bluebird is the first sign of spring. The bluebird spends winter in the south and moves north in early spring, often when the landscape is still cold and snowy. The bluebird makes its home near people, in farmlands, gardens, and orchards. It eats many kinds of harmful insects.

Chickadee, Black-Capped

The black-capped chickadee is a bird of the woods. It is named for the song it whistles—*chick-a-dee-dee-dee*. In the summer it eats insects, seeds, and berries; in winter it hunts among branches for the hidden eggs and cocoons of moths. It doesn't seem to mind cold weather and snow.

Bittern, American

The bittern lives in marshes among the bulrushes and cattails. When in danger, it stretches its neck straight up and freezes. The bird's body colors make it blend right into its surroundings. Bitterns eat fish, frogs, and other water creatures. Their call is a series of booming sounds.

Female

Male

Cardinal

The red cardinal, with his black mask, is well known in much of North America. But it is only the male bird that wears red—the female is a dull brown color. She too, however, has a jaunty peak of feathers on her head. Cardinals eat seeds and many kinds of harmful insects.

Condor, California

The California condor is the biggest bird in North America. It can glide for hours, peering down in search of the bodies of large dead animals on which to feed. There are so few of these big, spectacular birds left that they will probably soon be extinct.

Blackbird, Red-Winged

The red-winged blackbird lives in swamps, marshes, and at the edge of lakes and ponds. The female makes a basketlike nest of rushes, fastened to the stems of water plants. These birds eat a lot of harmful insects, but during their migration, they also eat some farm crops, especially corn.

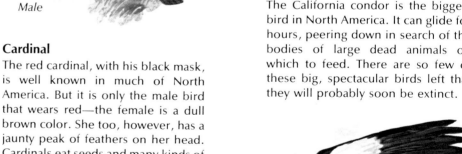

Coot, American

The American coot is found in shallow ponds and marshes where reeds and rushes grow. Its nest is a platform of dead water plants, woven together and fastened to the stalks of live plants. Coots eat the leaves, seeds, and roots of water plants as well as fish, snails, and insects.

Crow, Common

The common crow can make itself at home in woods, open country, and in cities and towns. It is a bold, clever creature that annoys farmers by eating young, green corn. But the crow also helps farmers by eating a great many harmful insects.

Curlew, Long-Billed

This curlew lives in meadows and prairies in western North America. There, it eats mostly grasshoppers, beetles, and caterpillars. When the curlew migrates, it often stops at lakes, rivers, and sandy beaches, where it eats small crabs, crayfishes, snails, and toads. It uses its long bill like a pair of tweezers.

Cuckoo, Yellow-Billed

The yellow-billed cuckoo is a bird of the forest. This is where it finds its favorite food—hairy tent caterpillars that often infest trees. Unlike the European cuckoo, which lays its eggs in the nests of other birds, the yellow-billed cuckoo builds a nest in a tree and cares for its own young.

Dove, Mourning

The word *mourning* means "sorrow," and the mourning dove was named for its call, which is a low, sorrowful-sounding *coo*. The mourning dove is common in open land throughout North America. It eats weed seeds and some insects.

Crossbill, Red

The bill of the red crossbill is a wonderful tool. The bird pushes its closed bill into the side of a pinecone, then opens the bill. This action rips open the cone, uncovering the seeds. The bird then plucks out the seeds with its scoop-shaped tongue. The red crossbill lives mostly in evergreen forests.

Egret, Snowy

The snowy egret lives near ponds, bays, and salt marshes in warmer parts of North America, and in South America. It sometimes fishes by dipping its foot into shallow water to stir up the mud on the bottom, then scurries about to snap up the small fish and crabs that come out.

Flicker, Common

The flicker is a kind of woodpecker. However, it gets a lot of its food off the ground instead of from trees. It is especially fond of ants, which it catches by poking its long, sticky tongue into ant nests. With its bill, the flicker drills a hole in an old dead tree or a telephone pole to make its nest.

Grebe, Pied-Billed

The pied-billed grebe is one of the best swimmers and divers of all birds. Grebes cannot easily walk on land, and although they are good fliers, they don't like to fly. They spend most of their lives in the waters of lakes, ponds, and rivers, where they eat fish, crayfish, and water insects.

Flycatcher, Scissor-Tailed

In summer, this bird makes its home in the southwestern United States. In winter, it moves to Mexico and Central America. When excited, it will open and close its long tail much like scissors, cutting. Although called a flycatcher, it eats mostly beetles, grasshoppers, and crickets.

Flamingo, American

Flamingos live in large flocks in muddy, shallow, rather salty lakes and lagoons. They poke their heads underwater to feed, straining the bottom mud through their bills to take out the many tiny plants and animals living in it.

Grouse, Ruffed

The ruffed grouse is a forest dweller. In early spring, a male ruffed grouse will pick a small patch of forest as his special territory. Standing on a log, he beats his wings rapidly in the air, making a drumming sound that warns other males away and calls for a female to come be his mate.

Guillemot, Black

The black guillemot lives along coasts in eastern North America and northwestern Europe. It is a fine swimmer and diver and a good flier, but it seldom flies more than a few feet above the water. The guillemot lays its eggs in crannies among the rocky sea cliffs. Its food is fish and shellfish.

Hawk, Red-Tailed

The red-tailed hawk lives throughout North America in open country dotted with groves of trees. It perches in trees, watching for prey, then glides silently down to snatch up a mouse, rat, rabbit, or other small creature. Red-tailed hawks make big, bulky nests near the tops of tall trees.

Jay, Blue

The blue jay has become a common sight in cities and towns. Like its cousin the crow, it is a bold and clever bird. It eats mostly acorns, nuts, seeds, and insects; but it will also eat young birds and bird eggs. Blue jays can imitate the calls of many other birds.

Kestrel, American

The American kestrel is a robin-size bird of prey belonging to the falcon family. It perches in trees and on telephone wires, watching for mice and insects, then dives like a flash, seizing its prey in sharp claws. Kestrels also capture sparrows and other small birds.

Gull, Herring

The herring gull lives along seacoasts and large rivers or lakes in the Northern Hemisphere. Although often called a sea gull, it never goes very far out to sea. It flies over the water, swooping down to the surface to snap up live or dead fish. Herring gulls also flock behind ships to dine on garbage thrown overboard.

Heron, Great Blue

The great blue heron generally lives by itself in a swamp. A skilled fisher, it stands motionless or slowly wades through shallow water watching for fish, frogs, or other water creatures. Then, the heron uses its bill to jab the prey.

Mallard

This duck is found in ponds, lakes, and streams in all parts of the Northern Hemisphere. It stays in the north until the lakes and ponds are almost ready to freeze, then it migrates southward. The mallard eats seeds, nuts, fruit, grass, small fish, tadpoles, and insects.

Kingfisher, Belted

The kingfisher dwells near rivers and streams. It sits high over the water and, when it spies a minnow or other small fish, dives straight into the water and seizes the prey in its bill. The kingfisher then flies to a nearby perch and swallows the fish headfirst.

Female

Male

Mockingbird

The mockingbird got its name because it can perfectly imitate, or *mock*, the calls of most other birds as well as the sounds of frogs, crickets, and even the noises of cars and sirens. The mockingbird lives mainly in the southern part of the United States and southward. It eats mostly berries and insects.

Magpie, Black-Billed

The magpie is a member of the crow family. Black-billed magpies live in small flocks in open country where there are few trees. They eat insects, mice, grain, fruit, and the remains of dead animals. They usually make their nests among the branches of thorny trees for safety.

Meadowlark, Eastern

As its name shows, the meadowlark lives in meadows and open country. It is a good friend to farmers, as it eats a great many of the insects that damage crops.

Nighthawk, Common

The nighthawk isn't really a hawk; it's a member of the family of birds known as nightjars. The nighthawk is a bird of open country, but it will also nest on the flat roof of a city building and hunt in city skies. It eats flying insects that it catches in midair.

Owl, Screech

The screech owl lives in open woodlands and forest clearings. By day, it stays hidden in holes in trees. At dusk, it comes out to perch over meadows and forest edges in search of mice. It also eats insects, bats, frogs, toads, and fish. Despite its name, the tiny owl's cry is more a whinnying wail than a screech.

Pelican, Brown

The brown pelican is a water bird that swims well and is a good flier. Its main food is fish, which it catches by diving into water with a loud smack that stuns nearby fish, making them easier to catch. The pelican scoops up the fish in its bill pouch, then swallows them.

Roadrunner

The roadrunner roams deserts and dry plains in southwestern North America. It can run as fast as 26 miles an hour, dodging and turning with ease at top speed. Its food is mainly insects, spiders, and scorpions, but it will also eat lizards and snakes—even poisonous ones!

Oystercatcher, American

The oystercatcher is a bird of the seashore and gets most of its food out of shallow water. Its long bill is a special tool for prying oysters off rocks and for opening up oyster shells.

Robin, American

For many people of North America, the sight of this bird is the first sign of spring. The robin begins moving northward and building a nest even when the weather is still cold and snowy. It seems to prefer living near people. It eats mostly worms in the summer and small fruits, berries, and insects during the winter.

Quail, Mountain

This bird lives in wooded, bushy places in the mountains of northwestern North America. It spends most of the time on the ground—feeding on leaves, flowers, buds, roots, and some insects. It can run quite fast and usually runs from danger instead of flying.

57

Shrike, Loggerhead

The loggerhead shrike is also called the butcher bird. For, just as a butcher hangs meat on hooks in his shop, the shrike hangs its prey—grasshoppers, lizards, and other small creatures—on thorns and broken branches. It does this to hold its food steady as it eats.

Sparrow, White-Throated

The white-throated sparrow spends its summers in the North, mostly in Canada. In winter it moves to the southern parts of the United States. A dweller of the woods and brushy woodlands, it scratches among the leaves on the ground in search of weed seeds, insects, and berries. It sings a high, melancholy whistle that sounds like *old Sam Peabody, Peabody, Peabody*.

Sparrow, House

The house sparrow, or English sparrow, likes to live near people. These little birds stay all year long in small flocks in towns, cities, and farm areas. They eat insects, seeds, bread, and other bits of food people leave lying about. Introduced into North America from Europe, they are now found from Alaska to South America.

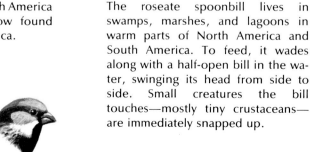

Female

Male

Spoonbill, Roseate

The roseate spoonbill lives in swamps, marshes, and lagoons in warm parts of North America and South America. To feed, it wades along with a half-open bill in the water, swinging its head from side to side. Small creatures the bill touches—mostly tiny crustaceans—are immediately snapped up.

Winter

Summer

Starling, European

Starlings are a common sight in cities and towns, where they are perfectly at home. They are bold, pushy birds that will rob other birds of food and nesting places. Starlings are also rather noisy and often cause annoyance to their human neighbors! As their name suggests, these birds were introduced into America from Europe.

Swan, Trumpeter

The trumpeter swan was given its name because its call sounds just like a high note played on a trumpet. The largest of all swans, the trumpeter feeds by sticking its head and neck underwater to nibble plants growing on the muddy bottom of a lake or pond.

58

Swift, Chimney

The chimney swift spends most of its life in flight. It eats flying insects that it catches in midair. It usually sleeps inside a chimney, clinging to the side with its tiny, hooklike feet and propping itself up with its stiff tail. It also builds its nest in a chimney.

Turkey

Turkeys eaten on holidays are raised on farms, but there are also flocks of wild turkeys living in some wooded parts of North America. These wild birds spend their days pecking insects, seeds, and wild berries off the ground. In the evening, they fly up into trees to spend the night.

Female

Male

Woodpecker, Downy

The downy woodpecker prefers to live in woodlands. With its chisel-bill, it drills into trees for hidden insects. It also eats the berries of some plants, such as poison ivy. To make a nest, the woodpecker drills a hole into an old, dead tree stump or branch.

Tern, Arctic

The Arctic tern lives on seacoasts and islands in the coldest parts of the world. Twice a year, it migrates a distance of 11,000 miles—from the Arctic to the Antarctic—then back again. It eats mostly fish, which it captures by diving straight down into the water, bill first.

Woodcock, American

The woodcock lives in moist, wooded places. It pushes its long slim bill down into the ground to feel for earthworms. When it finds one, it opens its bill tip slightly, even though the bill is buried in the earth, and swallows the worm.

Wren, House

The house wren is found throughout North America. It will make a nest in almost anything—a hole in a tree, a birdhouse, a tin can, a teapot, or even an old hat or boot! It eats many kinds of harmful insects.

Pronunciation Guide

Allosaurus	al-uh-SAW-ruhs		**kiwi**	KEE-wee
altricial	al-TRIHSH-uhl		**megapode**	MEHG-uh-pohd
anhinga	an-HIHNG-guh		**nocturnal**	nahk-TUHRN-uhl
Archaeopteryx	ahr-kee-AHP-tuh-rihks		**oriole**	OHR-ee-ohl
auk	AWK		**peregrine**	PEHR-uh-grihn
bobolink	BAHB-uh-lihngk		**phalarope**	FAL-uh-rohp
cassowary	KAS-uh-wehr-ee		**pheasant**	FEHZ-uhnt
cholla cacti	CHOY-uh KAK-ty		**pileated**	PY-lee-ayt-uhd
egret	EE-greht		**precocial**	prih-KOH-shuhl
emu	EE-myoo		**ptarmigan**	TAHR-mih-guhn
Gila	HEE-luh		**quail**	KWAYL
ginkgo	GIHNG-koh		**rhea**	REE-uh
guillemot	GEEL-uh-maht		**saguaro**	suh-WAHR-oh
gyrfalcon	JUHR-fal-kuhn		**skua**	SKYOO-uh
Hesperornis	hehs-puh-RAWR-nehs		**tarantula**	tuh-RANCH-uh-luh
Ichthyornis	ihk-thee-AWR-nihs		**tuatara**	too-uh-TAHR-uh

Index

Italic page numbers (for example: 8–9, 52) indicate color illustrations.

Emu, 14, 19

Falcon, 23, 28, 40, 50;
    peregrine, 18, 24, *25*, 34,
    40, 43
Flamingo, 14, 26, 35; American,
    . *54*
Flicker, common, *54*
Flycatcher, scissor-tailed, *54*
Food, 12, 14–16, 19, 20, 22–4,
    26–7, 38–40, 42, 44, 50
Frogmouth, 15

Goldfinch, 22
Goose, 14, 26, 30, 39; Canada, *45*
Grackle, 32
Grebe, 14, 19, 26, 35;
    pied-billed, *36*, *54*
Grosbeak, 22
Grouse, ruffed, 31, *54*
Guillemot, 34; black, *55*
Gull, 39, 40; herring, 30, 55;
    black-backed, 30

Hawfinch, 22
Hawk, 20, 24, 28, 50–1;
    red-tailed, 34, *55*; sparrow,
    34
Heron, 14, 18, 26, 40; great
    blue, *55*
Hornbill, 34
Hummingbird, 19, 22, 40;
    ruby-throated, 16, *17*, 18

Instinct, 46

Jay, blue, 24–5, *55*

Kestrel, American, *55*
Killdeer, 40, *41*
Kingfisher, 35; belted, *56*
Kiwi, 15, 19

Lapwing, 40

Lark, 14
Loon, 14

Magpie, 32; black-billed, *56*
Mallard. *See* Duck
Mating, 19, 30–2, 36–7, 44
Meadowlark, *37*, *56*
Megapode, 39
Merlin, 18
Migration, 44–7
Mockingbird, *56*

Nest, 23, 30; building of, 23, 32,
    33, 34–5, *36–7*
Nighthawk, 15, *56*
Nightjar, 15, 19;
    pennant-winged, 44

Oilbird, 15
Oriole, 32, *33*
Osprey, 24, 40
Ostrich, 12, *13*, 14, 19, 26
Ovenbird, 35, 36
Owl, 15, 20, 24, 28, 40, 50–1;
    barn, 48, *49*; burrowing, 35,
    37; elf, 34; great horned,
    29; screech, 34, *57*
Oystercatcher, 22; American, *57*

Partridge, 14, 30
Pelican, 14, 18, 22, 26, 40;
    brown, *57*
Penguin, 12, 14, 19; emperor,
    34; king, 31, 34
Petrel, 14
Petrel, dovey. *See* Shearwater,
    flesh-footed
Phalarope, 26
Pheasant, 14, 24, 26, 39
Pigeon, 24
Plover, 40; snowy, 34
Precocial birds, 38–40, 42
Preening, 23
Ptarmigan, willow, 31, 47

Quail, 39; mountain, 47, *57*

Rhea, 19
Roadrunner, 19, 23, 31, 40,
    50, *57*
Robin, 20, 27, 31, 32, 38, 39, 40;
    American, *57*

Sandpiper, 39
Sapsucker, 15
Secretary bird, 27
Shearwater, flesh-footed, 35
Shrike, loggerhead, *58*
Skua, 40
Sparrow, 20, 27, 32, 43, 51;
    house, *58*; white-throated,
    58
Spoonbill, 14; roseate, *58*
Starling, 46; European, *58*
Stork, European, 31
Swallow, 18, 46; barn, 36, *37*
Swan, 14, 26; trumpeter, *58*
Swift, 18, 19; chimney, 27, *59*;
    spinetailed, 19
Swiftlet, 36

Tailorbird, 22–3
Tern, 14, 40; Arctic, 47, *59*;
    royal, 34; sooty, 34
Thrush, 46
Turkey, wild, 26, *59*

Vulture, 42; king, 51; turkey,
    42

Waxwing, cedar, 51
Weaver, social, 37
Whip-poor-will, 35
Woodcock, 19, 22;
    American, *59*
Woodpecker, 26, 31, 32, 34, 47,
    50; downy, 32, *59*; Gila, 34;
    pileated, 20, *21*, 31, 32
Wren, house, 59

PRINTED IN U.S.A.